TIME SPENT AWAY

A collection of poems
c. 2010-2015

From California to Colorado and many places in between.

Copyright © 2018 by Tyler Lee Schaefer

Original art and layout by Emily Poulin

All rights reserved. This book or any portion thereof may not be reproduced or used in any manner whatsoever without the express written permission of the author except for the use of brief quotations in a book review.

Printed in the United States of America

First Printing, 2018

ISBN 978-0-578-42872-7

www.tylerschaefer.com

I dedicate this collection to the people and places that took me in along the way. To the sour concoctions we shared and the silly things we smoked. Thank you for the beds, couches, and floors you offered me along the way.

You are the letters that fill this space.

TIME SPENT AWAY
somewhere outside of Las Vegas, NV. c. 2010

Into the desert before the sun was.
Where neon buzzes like whiskey whispers
The atmosphere radiating through bones
Through walls, and windows, and faces.

Where Indian casinos stand awkwardly
Like a thirteen year old girl
Trying on makeup for the first time.
Too much blush on her cheeks
Eyeliner for miles, lipstick billboards.

They look uncomfortable and exploited
Made to stand there for the white man's pleasure
Like a door that revolves, or a cut that festers.

Little girls that lead me deeper into the desert
Toward their much older cousin
The unnatural oasis of lights and glass
A city of sin.
I've got no time to stop.
No time to consider the choice.
Just the truck, myself and the road.
Just all my shit in a box, in the back.
Into the desert, as to go through the desert.
I aim to hit Colorado by nightfall

time spent away

This marks the longest I've yet driven alone
The farthest I've been by my own doing.
Where the cactus stand up, dry as a bone
To the sound of tires eaten by asphalt's chewing.

Behind me are the ghosts of things once loved,
Behind me stands that goddamned church
Behind me are the stains of rotten, bad blood
Behind me is a holiest of holies sized hurt

May these mountains offer shelter, a cleft or two
And may my pace be quicker than my demons run.

It hurts like hell to leave, but what can I do?

I fear I had no choice, for my restlessness weighs a ton
No more tricks, no more ideas, and with nothing to say

The road calls to me asking to take me far,

       far

           away.

tl schaefer

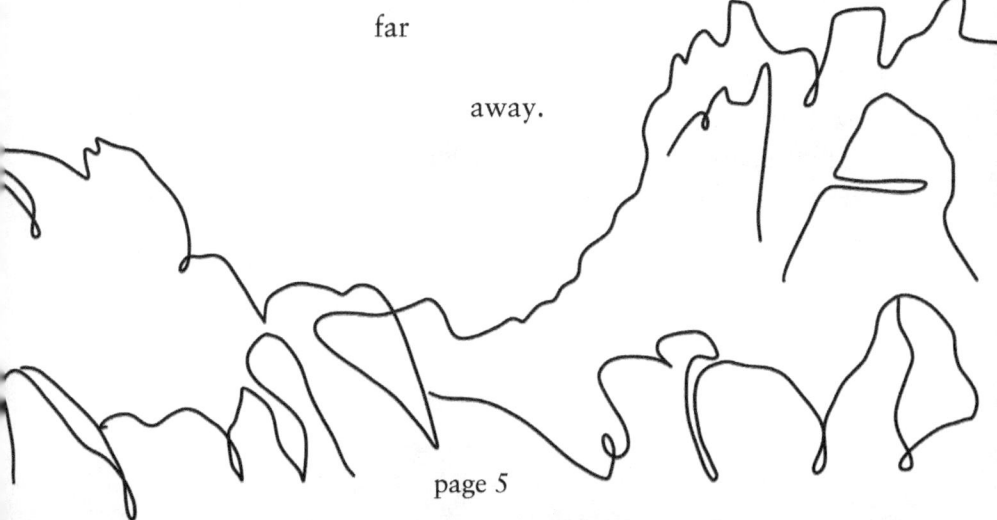

RED ROOF INN
Gallop, NM c. 2010

Cactus, asphalt, lost hubcaps
Hiking trails, rest stops and folded maps
May I learn to speak like the trees
And yell like the breeze

Red rocks, white sand, rolling plains
Retro houses, abandoned schools and sewage drains

Eureka! I've abandoned the golden state
And rolled into the land of enchantment
Of different signs, a different license plate
As I drive forward in my advancement
The sky stretches as it yawns over the country
Lifting arms towards the heavens, forever long
My heavy eyes looking for a sodium lamp vacancy
Invited by the sojourner's siren, the highway's song
I've crawled all the way to Gallup, New Mexico
From Los Angeles, from the sprawling chimera
Miles have begun their carving, but I've got more to go

As I search for a room, in this distance I'm suddenly aware of

Home causes nothing but pain when this far.
Home must become where my two feet are.

time spent away

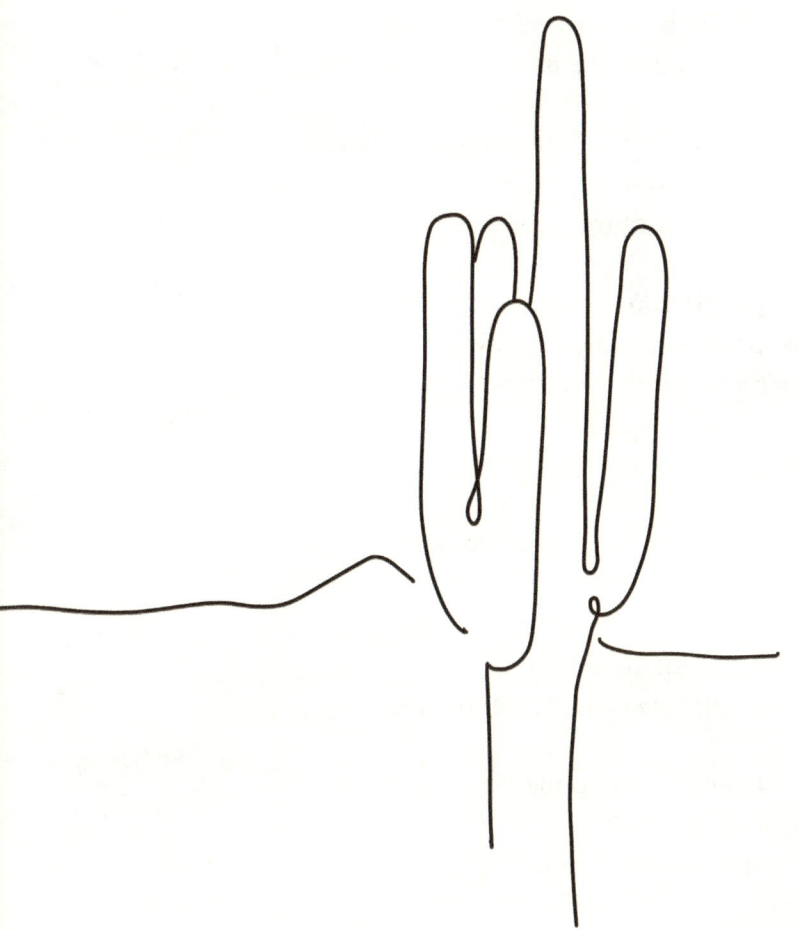

tl schaefer

DESERT SNOW
somewhere outside of Flagstaff, AZ. c.2012

There is snow in the desert
Up on the hills, white and confusing.
Just like you, just like us.

You guys live in a building made of blocks
Where it's part of your tuition
Where it's part of the experience.

Some people you grow up with
Some people you know forever
I don't know if that matters.

I don't know if any of it matters.
Like how I adored you as a kid
Like how it just never worked out.

But I've got my toes in the highway
I feel it pulling me away
The asphalt tide is dragging me east.

School never stuck to me
Not many things have
Not many people either.

I think I want you to tell me to stop,
To stay the night
Sleep on the floor, or the bed
In that house of blocks
Where nothing is confusing

time spent away

Not childhood, nor the friends we make
Nor the passions we may be moments from
Or miles between.
Not the snow in the desert
Nor how it contradicts the landscape.

I'll leave as soon as we get quiet
As soon as our plates are empty
As soon as it makes sense.

I'll sleep on the side of the road
And you in a house of bricks
Both looking for clarity.

BUDDY BACK WEST
Englewood, CO. c. 2014

Summer was slowly eaten by fall
Autumn went in a similar way
As the trees stood naked and tall
The grass taken, now the new snow lay
Memories arrived as a backwards migration

Scars begin to serve as pleasure or as a photograph
As we speak of reunion, pregnant with anticipation
And as we recall, recount, revisit, and honestly laugh
In my mind, we're walking back into that Green Parrot
We'll put a handful of quarters on the pool table
Stagger up to the bar, request a pitcher and share it.

That summer was born a legend and died a fable

I tell you brother, of my being blessed
To be your buddy back west.

time spent away

tl schaefer

OF THE ROADS TAKEN
Leadville, CO. c. 2012

Of the roads calling that dip
Freeways down into the outside night
Backflipping, they yield, splinter and rip
They all offer up direction an opportunistic trip
Some are called wrong, some known as right

Though they are described in books
Or through missing-toothed stories of old men
They are understood by babbling brooks
Or in solitude with the nakedness of the woods
These diving highways of possibility that wend

In my youth I had become enamoured
With their bend, the shape of their curves
Took to the asphalt, foot down and hammered
Serpents, I let them eat me and was overpowered
This is their pain, the intersection that occurs.

Of the roads taken, I ponder the ones neglected
Where I had merged, exited, or parked entirely
Where I should have plowed but deflected
And yet of all these ways I've inspected

I fear the most, the road yet inside of me.

time spent away

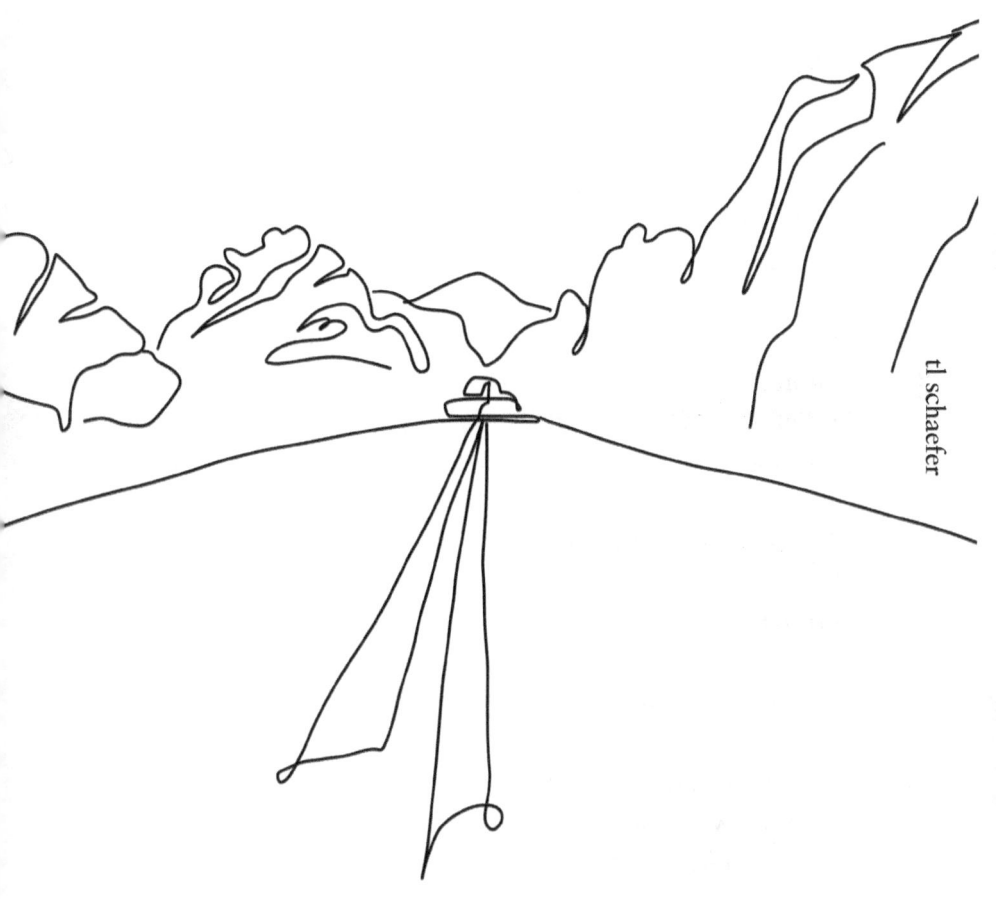

tl schaefer

JUMPIN' GOOD GOATS
Buena Vista, CO. c. 2010

There is a pasture in this valley's throat
Inside that green patch
A tribe of goats are tended to
Protected and brought up.

The goats look like little, white
Specks of mold on a green apple
They look as white islands,
In a mossy tide.

When I drive up to Leadville, I see the shepherds
I don't know if they call them that
When they tend to goats
But that is what I've come to call them.

They make me think of certain men
Of a certain cloth
I don't know if I can call them holy
When they neglect the flock,
To tend to themselves.

I think of that carpet on the floors
And the way your voice sounds
When spoken through a microphone
It has a different power
When it is behind closed doors.

time spent away

Sometimes when I drive by that white flock
I ask God why those goats
Get protected better than I did.
I ask God why some men
Like to molest little boys.

Why my shepards were as wolves.
I ask him why I needed to run away
All the way to this valley
I ask him why I still can't run fast enough.

The wind whips my face as I drive
And the radio is playing something.
I guess that's as good an answer
I will get.

Perhaps God's voice is actually yours,
Played through that damned microphone.

Maybe it's just a drove of stupid goats,
That don't mean shit to anyone.

OUTSIDE THE GREEN PARROT
Buena Vista, CO. c. 2012

I have spoken with a tweaker on a bike.
With priests, sinners, young, and old alike
With young women who hold babies on their hips
And cowboys with tobacco stuffed in their lips
I have met foreigners from distant lands
Heard the bankrupt hope in a drunk's plans
Heard stories from brainwashed fanatics
And slept in unkempt beds with fellow addicts
Compared palms with a gypsy or two
And sang along with those ever-blue.
Met a man who worked in the oil fields
And his beautiful sister he forever shields
Broke bread with the rich and educated
And listened slow with the old and desecrated
Talked in circles with a couple river rats
And complimented them on their trucker hats
All different, but in the same way we to drift sleep
All different, but all in fact someone's sheep
Some of us odd and alone from the pack
Some of us white red yellow turquoise or black.

Outside this bar, I've sparked a smoke or two
In the snow, the rain, and perfect weather too.

I don't know what I want, it's true
But this bar reminds me of you.

time spent away

tl schaefer

TRAILER PARK BLUES
Buena Vista, CO. c. 2012

Dirt roads and dirty hands
Gripping at something just out of sight

All the doors here have self-closing hinges
As we drink, our mouths start to lose theirs
They fall off and land in the dirt.

The pilsner heavyweight and sativa philosopher
Are in their plastic lawn chairs
And I am sitting between them
In this trailer park, in the dirt
Where no one dresses like me
Where no one talks like me
The only thing familiar to me
Are the lights and how they buzz
Or how we buzz.

There's a girl here and she's beautiful in a way
That is unique to this place.
In a way that makes me feel like a foreigner
In a white man's country.

There's a girl here and she's as far away
As far as can be and in this dirt,
I understand why.

time spent away

In this dust, this trailer park
We are all transplants.
From back east, or over west.
From the town below us
Or the big bad city with its cars and rules.
We are a family of trimmings
Cut and tossed out.

And the blood that binds us
Is the feeling,
That no one really wants to be here

    In this dirt.

tl schaefer

DAVE KELLY'S RANCH
Buena Vista, CO. c. 2010

There is a ranch on a knoll
It lives at the mountain's icy feet
The sky, it looks right through your soul
Sunlight laying over it as a radiant bedsheet
A four-legged duo to play fetch with indefinitely
Two lakes, Canadian geese, and an insect swarm

Inside laughter, food, and taxidermy
Making the coldest of persons warm

Elk steaks over charcoal
Beer that tastes like grass

There is a ranch on a knoll
Where heaven and Earth contrast
I think the stones are trying to say something, crying out
With each sunset as a hot lava iceberg or dying shout.

THE RED HEELER
Buena Vista ,CO. c. 2014

A red Heeler she is my good sir
A good red Heeler, that is her

Her litter was two red and four blue
Her litter, all healthier and bigger too

Suppose that's how I made my pick
Suppose it's because she didn't stand a lick

Both of us travel, the two oceans we've seen
Both of us, many a highway in between

My sweet pup doesn't mind me when I drink
My sweet pup doesn't cringe when I stink

Sweet Sasha, my lovely dear.
Sweet Sasha, my Heeler true and sincere.

time spent away

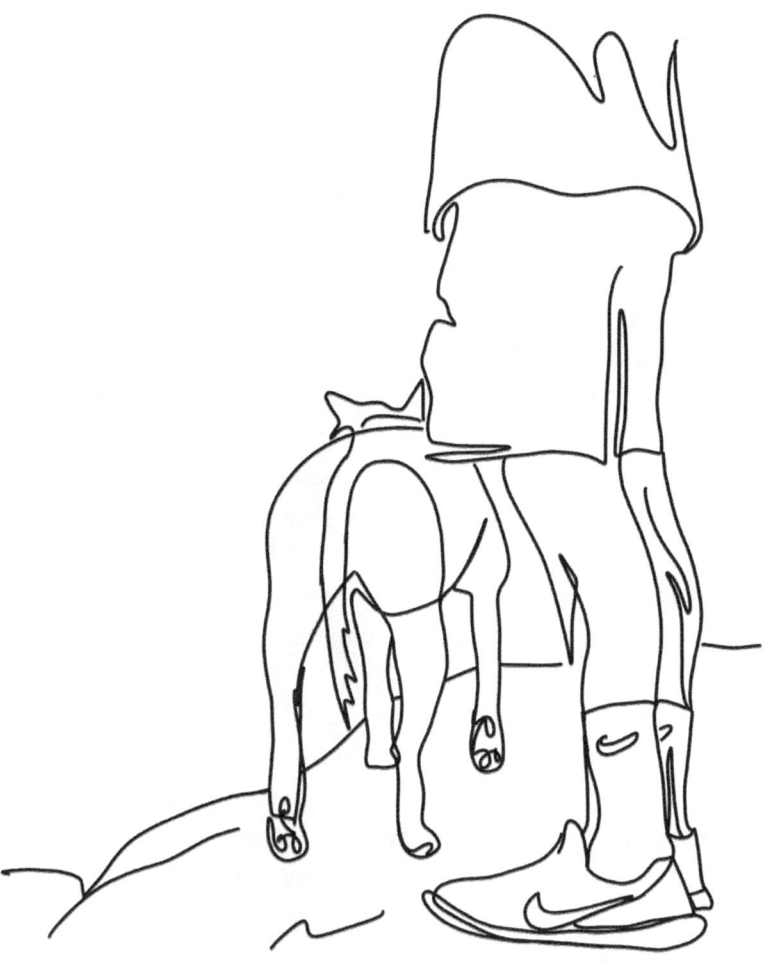

tl schaefer

SHUMAN
Buena Vista ,CO. c. 2014

The weekend is over so I'm drinking water
Alone, in some parking lot
I cry for your sister and her daughter
I heard that she had passed
And I am haunted by questions, the ones I never asked

Summer is half dead and soon every last tree
Alone, in some parking lot, I wonder if you still think of me
These years have stung, they've made me tough
But you have your husband, and I get drunk before lunch.
I can't help but think of that night two years ago
When we escaped town, drove past that mine though the snow
Everyone in the truck had whisky in their lungs
Everyone in the truck had youth pressed through teeth and tongues.
I was in the passenger seat for the ride back
It was the first time in that elevation I'd thrown some back
You held my hand from behind my seat
While everyone tried to decide where to eat.

The weekend is over, and I've got nothing but the next to chase
I've got only memories and outlines to trace
I'm sorry for your sister and the accident she was in
I'd reach out, but I don't know where to begin.
There is no getting back those chances, those times
There is no rereading the plot, understanding the lines
But that's okay, I am starting to learn
I exist only on weekends.

    I'm just waiting my time, my turn.

time spent away

tl schaefer

ANOTHER SUMMER
Denver, CO. c. 2013

The house is full again
People I sort of know
Falling asleep, my breath is gin
Laying down, my breath is slow

Life is a bitch, bitten and cold
My back is sore, hands rough
My soul is tired and feelin' old
My soul is tired of bein' tough

Been chasing Jesus and hope
Right now I am homesick and half drunk
Honey, I am at the end of my rope
Honey, I am a ship that is sunk

I am so tired of sleepin' alone
I am so tired of this goddamned phone
I am tired of my heart being stone
I am tired of the sound of its groan

I am tired and just want to be home.

time spent away

tl schaefer

FOREST FIRES
Colorado Springs, CO - Riverside, CA. c. 2012 - 2015

The sky makes it known to the clouds
That have overstayed their welcome
So they leave.

With them they take the rain
Like a reluctant child in a divorce
The clouds take it away by the ear
Rain, after all, has never been independent.

In both their absences and under the sky's naked face
Heat and dryness squat in the vacancies
Together the duo eat the colors of the hills
They drink the moisture
Like kings.

Bears carved out of wood hold signs
Or rather they hold dials
Or rather they hold colors
They tip us off to the danger.

It's just a change of seasons
The order of things we know
So we don't think past, or before it
And accept it.

It's just fire season.
It happens every year.

time spent away

Eventually all these things will give birth to the season's namesake
It'll starts off so small, big things often do.
Find the parallels, smell the metaphor.
Cliché.

Red will evolve from being a color
It'll learn to breathe, splinter and dance.
Orange shall follow the same, the two reproducing
Their lineage as one of variance.

Animals, if they can, will pour out of the forest
Seeking refuge, they'll dart
Horns, hooves, wings, claws
They have always feared the fire
For what it's worth, so do I.

The fire season fears nothing
It's only a season, after all
You can't expect that much of it.

~~~~~~

The nerve endings in my brain look like the bare branches of a twenty-six-year-old oak tree.

My fire seasons started at eight years old and not a cloud has been seen since. Grass the color of dirt and the wind like salt in a wound. It must be that time of year again.

It's the smell that really gets to me. I can smell it on people's words. It pours out of the hollowness of their eyes. They hide their soul like a burn victim would hide their scarred skin. The clan of turtlenecks in July, the T-shirts in the swimming pool and camouflage painted faces are they. They have adapted to hide the scars but it's the smell that is a bit more tricky.

I know this smell, for I smell it on my own breath. My clothes hide the burns, but the smell pushes out. Filling every empty space, touching everything.

We have different words for these fires. Each one slightly different in hue, but similar in the way they burn. They call mine post-traumatic stress disorder. PTSD for short. They usually use the acronym, it's easier. Post-traumatic stress disorder is a bit of a mouthful.

While most earned that condition in the battlefield, I earned my in a bedroom. I was not in uniform when I earned my badges but I received my commendation the same. Thus the fire was sparked. The arsonist wasn't a careless cigarette, but instead a very intentional young man. My innocence was the kindling and, goddamnit burnt quick.

The seasons come and go and I have lived through many of them. Hope is the way life starts to grow back. Misery is when the flames lick it back away. Horror is knowing that both will happen. Again, and again.

―――

The sky apologized to the clouds
And with the clouds came rain
With the rain came growth
The scorched earth slowly pushed out life.

While the terrain never looked the same again
There was something tenacious about it
More beautiful
More vivid.

Something that said, "in spite of"
Though it took so much more effort
Though the ground would always hold the memory.

The first flower that bloomed
Well, I think the red in its petals
Burns in a way
No fire ever could.

MANSFIELD/DELAWARE
Englewood, CO. c. 2013

Been sleeping funny on a hard bed
Been eating poorly, and drinking like mad

Sometimes with an ache in my cloudy head
Sometimes melancholy, sometimes glad

But, a house isn't a home to some
But, now a home feels miles from me

The outside lights sleep talk in a hum,
The Denver horizon is all that I can see

I think a monster lives underneath this foundation
I think a monster hides inside my chest

Are we friends? Made so by situation?
Are we lost together? Abandoned by the rest?

Yet we light one to share,
Somewhere between Mansfield and Delaware.

time spent away

tl schaefer

FLYING J
Riverside, CA. c. 2015

Memories drove towards me like an eighteen-wheeler when I got your message.
You and your cruelty.
Nightmare Before Christmas tattoos,
You were my nightmare.
Full steam, pissing smoke from both stacks
Like an eighteen-wheeler leaving that Flying J.

Nicotine, marijuana smoke, and cheap beer stained the kitchen walls
Felon dads, losing teeth and paycheck-to-paycheck
That house was hell, best as I have ever known it
Hell was a house in Englewood, Colorado.

I can still hear your slurred bullshit
I can see the void behind your eyes
Feel the sting of your life
I am still scared of you.

"Hey man, I miss you, how have you been?
I'm still up to the same stuff, yeah still in Denver,
My son is fine, haven't seen him since Christmas,
His mom is a bitch,
I am down in California, supposed to leave today,
But my truck is broken down."

time spent away

Your truck was always fucked up.

Back then, both of our cocaine noses
Made us into clowns.
As I thought you could help me
As you thought I could help you
Cinnamon-flavored whiskey
Brought the devil out
And he was welcome to stay.

I don't know how to tell you
That I still remember
That old farmer with giant hands
Hands the size of God's
Who sold amphetamines, who kept us up
For nights on end.
The blowtorch and glass
The sorrow and insanity.

I don't know how to tell myself now
I was just trying to survive.
I don't know how to tell you
That I survived.

A brief exchange, words that are so weak
Weak in the way I used to be
I had no worth then, I think you always knew that
I think you still know that.

I want to grab a beer with you, I really do,
Want to be friends again, talk that same shit
I want to grab fire and feel it as cold
You want to ignore the smoldering crater.

time spent away

My hate is a giant, and it steps on you
It crushes me, and everyone else I know.
My justification is found in his claws, as he tears you apart.
My hate drove me from my home and into your arms.
My hate makes me weak in a way you know.

As you cross state lines, I cross my heart
And hope to die
And promise to try and forgive you
I want to believe that someday you will change
But habits formed for many years are seldom forgot

Just like you and your booze.

    And me with my hate.

time spent away

tl schaefer

ASTRONAUTS
Gunnison, CO. c. 2013

We paid ten bucks for each small square of paper,
And I've held them all week
Inside my freezer.

We shot pool and shot through a pitcher,
And the beer made us brave,
Inside a bar older than most.

We put those papers under our tongue,
And went for a walk into the night,
Inside our mouths, the paper dissolved.

Theory became fact and fact is fragile,
Like lines and shapes, they just are.
As the LSD ate through the membranes,
That held my mind down,
I wondered about God.
I wondered if I'm getting closer or further,
Or if it even works like that.

We talked to some skeezer in the liquor store.
Trading paper and coins for tall cans,
There were points made on the free market,
Something about capitalism.
Who cares?

Trippin.

time spent away

Someone asks where we are going,
"Where there is ground under our feet."
A voice speaks into the night,
Not sure whose, probably my own.

We fried all night, ended up at the park,
Listened to Pink Floyd,
This is what you do.

We talked all night, got to the heart of it all,
Listened to similar voices,
This is what happens.

The next weekend we got us some mushrooms,
To do the same thing,
To talk about the same things,
To wonder about the same God.

I guess this is what I do now.
I turn my brains inside out and show them to the sky,
Begging for something to see it.
Begging for a line, begging for an answer.

With paper under our tongues,
Or the fungus in our bowels,
We are astronauts here.
Stuck in the pull of a gravity,
Neither one of us want.

RED ROCKS
Denver, CO. c. 2012

You sit as a jewel hung from a mountain range necklace,
Pacific saline strands of hair due west and out of state,
I drove to this jewel alone, across her desert face,
Up the passes and down a craggy and frosted nape.

A locket of blistering crimson proof, jagged and colossal.
Product of a fierce disagreement inside the Earth's pelvis,
Fingers of minerals press from your throat, each tonsil.
You are tenacious from each point to each crevasse.

When night falls, we climb together into your womb,
Where strings vibrate and drums beat to arouse apparitions.

Tectonic beast of cardinal and slab your music rises as perfume.
Calling forth pilgrims and the vagabond into similar submissions.
I reached for you as neither, and still yet a boy searching in vain,

You reached back with red rocks, whispering through the rain.

time spent away

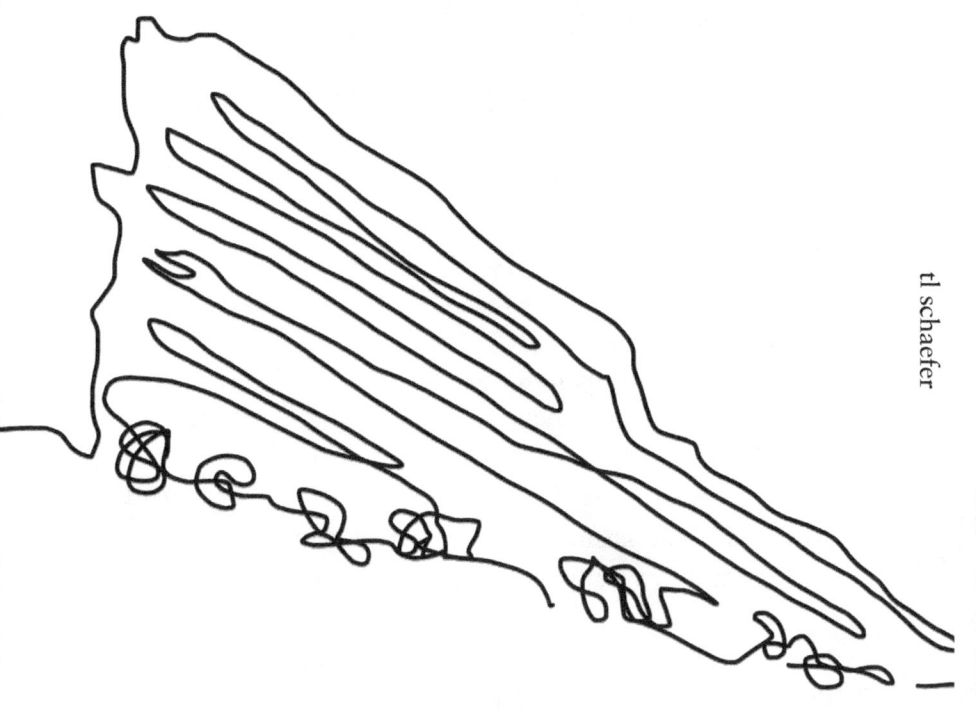

tl schaefer

SOBO
Denver, CO. c. 2014

Jerseys on the walls, the liquor tastes like Christmas,
With a small bite in the stockings, a small flame,
As it rests in my belly, burning, I forget the distance,

Warm inside where booze lubricates the dialogue pistons,
A bar to hold our elbows and burdens the same,
Jerseys on the walls, the liquor tastes like Christmas,

An arsenal of Czech beauties, blonde ballistics,
Shooting looks, grazing backs, the delicate game,
As it rests in my belly, burning, I forget the distance,

Where fanatics conjoin to celebrate persistence,
And persons become united by a team's name,
Jerseys on the walls, the liquor tastes like Christmas,

Dialogue blends and splinters through present and past tense,
Baptized in the saturation of it, restored and made sane,
As it rests in my belly, burning, I forget the distance,

I love you for how you offer to smuggle me from existence,
Be it an hour or a day, be you freedom or chain,
Jerseys on the walls, the liquor tastes like Christmas,
As it rests in my belly, burning, I forget the distance.

time spent away

tl schaefer

TACO JOHN'S
Rawlins, WY. c. 2014

The semi trucks snore as we all sleepwalk,
At eighty miles an hour and across state lines,
Exhaust brakes with a throaty gurgle, antilock.

Wyoming has only ever been a place,
For me to drive through or drop off,
Too quick for a friend, escaped the embrace.

We parted ways in a Taco John's, silent,
And I had a drive back to Denver before me,
To a place like a home, perhaps beside it.

Your brunette hair will be on my pillows back there,
And the sheets will probably still smell like you,
But it's just old perfume and strands of brown hair.

When I drove out, three days ago, I had hope,
Perhaps we'd fall in love, in a weekend's time,
In a passion of romance together, we'd elope.

Instead, we used our bodies as kindling,
For the inferno of loneliness we both hold,
Fooled by it all, the fleshy swindling.

I don't blame us, it gets freezing here.
The kind of cold that gives you habits,
Or a look in your eyes, or a fear.

time spent away

My bed will be empty, and the fire will continue to lick
At wounds packed with each other's sweat and salt,
Willing to give away everything but commitment.

We drove opposite directions until out of sight,
And as the sun died, I felt nothing,
Tail lights as fireflies in the pitch of night.

Just outside of Cheyenne, half my journey logged,
I stopped for a smoke and a coffee,
Watching the trucks play leapfrog.

Pulling at the smoke and against the car door,
I felt a sadness, as if we'd fooled each other the same,
Both holding back something, both needing more.

Back on the road, I swim down this river of asphalt.
There is a sadness in my glacier chest, frozen numb,
And I'd love to blame you for it, but that's not your fault.

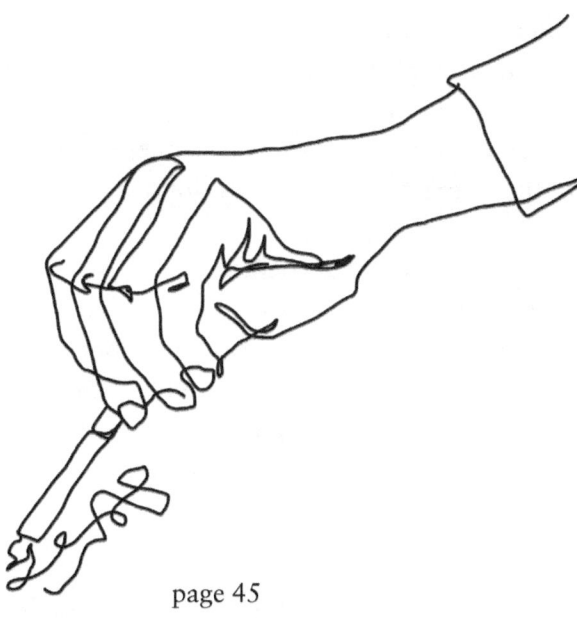

THE BLUE BENCH
Denver, CO. c. 2014

We sat around the waiting room as pelts,
as the skins of what we were.

No one makes eye contact, no one says a word, we just wait.
Pelts don't make small talk, they don't shoot smiles, they just
hang on walls.

Trappers and hunters, with massive hands and empty eyes,
With rifles and snares, flinging boiling lead or breaking leg bones.
In the silence they stalk, camouflaged as family, friend, or pastor.

We sit in the old house they repurposed into a clinic,
For those like me, the pelts, with invisible wounds,
With broken brain bones, who dream terrors and sweat,
The taxidermied tribe of the raped and sexually abused.

I can't help but notice, I can't help but feel the discomfort,
From my own fear of becoming as the camouflaged man,
Who plunged into me, as a knife pulled up into my sternum,
To clean out anything innocent, to empty me of structure,
On the river's bank he left my guts, all of them tiny as a child's.

I can't help but notice, I am the only man in this place.
Am I the only one that was too stupid to see the blind?
Was my gait uniquely clumsy as it stepped into the jaws?
There is a woman sitting next to me, I can feel her eyes,
I want her to know that I'm not like them, they skinned me too,
But I stay quiet, and in that way I take it. Like a man.

time spent away

I think back to the times I took shelter inside of the shade,
The jacuzzi-chested, itchy faced, carpet bombing shade,
Of the all powerful and understanding poppy flower,
The opium foxhole, retaining walls of pills, pillows of powder.
My God, my God, why hath thou forsaken me?

I'd give anything for just a lick of the morphine's favor,
Or to be anywhere but this fucking house of pelts,
Away from these people who want to help me,
Give me the briar patch. I know the pain. I understand it.

Yet I stay in this room designated for those waiting.
I can't go back to the briar patch, I know it deeply.
The fall would kill me. I'd never get untangled.

Instead I offer up what I have left, with both hands
A skin from an animal I used to know, used to be.
It's all I've had to keep warm with. It's what kept me alive.

ROCK LEDGE RANCH
Colorado Springs, CO. c. 2014

Young enough to be able to hold both parents in its sky
The day is cutting its teeth on humanity's bustle.

Early morning fog conjured by dawn's dying wish
Seeps between the mountain's toes and into the park.
They migrate sleepily up the Rockies, offering a clearing
As if the steam of a bathroom gave way to a portal
While she is stepping out, her shoulder blades still dripping.

I'm sneaking glances at her nakedness.

Color falls like a poncho over the whole scene
While the sun, as a lone rider, gallops into town.
Twirling a hand rolled cigar in its teeth, drawn back lips.
Six shooter protruding from the hip.

Oranges from Moroccan spice markets pepper the peaks
Dusted heavily in each dip of the bluffs.
Veins of red, not quite that of blood, but of rust
Topped by a white known to be snow.
All their skeletons cast in a purple that evades,
Defies, and ridicules description.
Living outside of words and their abilities.

The fog clears from the ranch,
And there is a forest of deep green that contrasts.
As I stand in the clearing, by the old house.
The one with a foundation made of riverstones.
From a time long forgotten yet romanticised.

time spent away

For a moment I am outside of reality,
As colors call from a place far away and of eternity.
My mind is baffled and haunted by beauty,
As I try to understand its origin or genealogy.
Who carries its leash? Who holds the key?

Someone holds it and someone sets it free.
In all my talent, all my cunning, and ability
I can only call it heavenly.

    A heaven I hope to see.

tl schaefer

ABITA
Denver, CO. c. 2014

You accepted me, in totality, ugliness and flaws
And at times, you stopped my world with your paws

Home is not something to romanticize
Especially when home has a wet nose
Folded ears, and two brown eyes

Denver's mountain teeth
Her cold breath and river feet

Lysergic acid diethylamide and psilocybin skies,
The wounds that thawed and froze
And a boxer small for her size

We were both sold cheap, a price reduce,
Fought through the void, survived abuse,

I left you both, went west,
Now I hoard the memories left,
As death makes you rest,
You slept in my empty room when I moved,
Unable to say goodbye and removed.

You were home to a broken man,
With a stormy head, shaky hand,
Tired, fearful, and emotionally jammed,

My angel, with a flattened face,
Full of mercy. Full of grace.

time spent away

tl schaefer

CITRUS
Riverside, CA. c. 2015

Wrought iron against the rocks, palm trees waving,
A raincross pressed into the concrete curb, paralyzed,
I understand these roads, I know this paving,
As I see again my dreams, my longing materialized,
A canal runs through the center of it all, with a green gut,
Magnolia trees and eucalyptus outline its winding shape,
Grapefruit trees that hold softballs, are fed by the cut,
Oranges and lemons too, reach with roots for their take,
An old hotel with cement walls and two macaws in an ancient cage,
Still holds the lights for the Christmas I had a few days ago missed,
The familiar soothes the wounds but I only notice the change,
And the feeling is somewhere between sour and sweet - as citrus,
As I wonder if I actually arrived back home or elsewhere,
Straddling states with memories,
    feeling neither here nor there.

time spent away

tl schaefer

TIME SPENT AWAY REDUX
Riverside, CA. c. 2015

The morning sun's fingers stretched up
Pushed over the hills and into the sky
And I'm runnin' back home on pressed luck
Diesel fumes, and days gone by

Goddamn, the memories sit like school kids
Bumping shoulders in my mind, biting tongues
And holding the heart inside my cruel ribs
Goddamn we had some good ones.

In this way I leave nothing behind me
Shedding youth's romantic soft skin
And now forever adopted, my vagabond family
The Rocky Mountains crooked, frost grin,

I was in the desert when the night conceded to day,

    Made, at last, into a man by the

        time

  I

      spent

away.

time spent away

tl schaefer

A PARTING WORD

Of the time that was spent away was not all easy,
nor was it all hard.

There is a beauty in the open road never known until one braves it in solitude. Universities of wisdom offer enrollment to those sleeping on floors. Studying on couches. The ones invited into the stranger's home, unafraid in taking the steps.

Unique to the open road there is a pain. A horror exists in the process of exploration. Unkind is the nature of the world we share, especially to those in search of new things. Especially the ones who chase after beauty.

May you accept them both.
May you exist in the contrast.
Use them to create with.
Do so with conviction.

Spend time away.

— tl schaefer

www.ingramcontent.com/pod-product-compliance
Lightning Source LLC
Chambersburg PA
CBHW022000290426
44108CB00012B/1150